THE POWER POINTS OF OVERCOMING WITCHCRAFT IN THE CHURCH

Tawana T. Thomas

Diligence Publishing Company
Bloomfield, New Jersey

The Scripture in this book is from the King James Version and the New International Version.

THE POWER POINTS OF OVERCOMING WITCHCRAFT IN THE CHURCH

Copyright © 2018 Tawana T. Thomas
c/o Diligence Publishing Company
P.O. Box 2476
Bloomfield, New Jersey

All Rights Reserved

No part of this book may be reproduced in any form without the written permission from the publisher except for brief passages included in a review.

To contact Tawana Thomas to preach or speak at your church, organization, seminar or conference email:
tawana_thomas@rocketmail.com

THE POWER POINTS OF OVERCOMING WITCHCRAFT IN THE CHURCH

ISBN: 978-1-7331353-3-7

Printed in the United States

TABLE OF CONTENTS

Acknowledgements 5
Introduction: The Three Realms 7
1: Normal Abnormalities 13
2: The Things That God Hates 19
3: The Spirit of Jezebel 23
4: Spiritual Wives and Spiritual Husbands 35
5: Strongholds 41
6: Witchcraft 45
7: Spiritual Authority 55
8: Weapons of Warfare 59
9: Overcoming Witchcraft 73
10: Break the Curse: Family 81
11: Break the Curse: Finances 87
12: Break the Curse: Poverty 89
13: Break the Curse: Restoration 91
14: Break the Curse: Healing 93
15: Break the Curse: Hindrances 95
16: Redemptive Power: Seven Promises 97
17: Redemptive Power: The Lord's Prayer 99
18: Redemptive Power: Overcoming Witchcraft 101
Epilogue: New Beginnings 103
Bibliography 113
About the Author 117
Order Information 121

ACKNOWLEDGEMENTS

A very special thank you to all of you that prayed with me, counselled me and have been a listening ear. Thank you for being my strength and present help in troubled times. May our Heavenly Father bless you all tremendously, beyond your imagination. In the name of Jesus Christ. AMEN! AMEN! AMEN!

LOVE ALWAYS
Tawana

INTRODUCTION

The Three Realms

Where did this all begin? Does the spiritual world have access to the natural world? Does the natural world have access to the spiritual world? Yes, God needs your body as a dwelling place. He needs you as a vessel. If He needs you as a vessel, a dwelling place, how much more does Satan need a body to function through? It is illegal for a spirit to operate in the natural realm without permission. For example, when we pray the Lord's Prayer "thy kingdom come, thy will be done on earth as it is in Heaven" we are giving God permission to function and to operate freely in our lives, in the natural realm.

The three realms are the first heaven, the second heaven and the third heaven.

The first heaven is what we see with our natural eyes; we see the sky, the clouds, the birds in the air and airplanes. God, the creator of the universe, assigned earth as man's domain. In the book of Genesis 1:7-8 it says, "And God called the firmament Heaven." God has given man dominion over the earth: over the sea, the air and every living creature upon the earth (Genesis 1:26). Mankind created civilizations, established government, and cultivated the land as well as landed on the moon.

The second heaven is the universe, the stars, and the solo system. This is the realm that Satan has rule over. In this realm resides the principalities, rulers of darkness, powers, demonic forces, familiar spirits, and spiritual wickedness; psychics witches and warlocks operate in the occultic realm. Satan also has dominion over the first heaven (man's domain) *Therefore rejoice ye heavens, and ye that dwell in them. Woe to the inhabitants of the earth and of the sea! For the devil is come down unto you having great wrath. Because he knoweth that he hath but a short time"* Revelations 12:12.

Lastly there is the third heaven which is God's domain. We find in the book of Revelation 4:2 *"and immediately I was in the spirit: and behold, a throne was set in heaven and one sat on the throne."*

Genesis 28:12 *"Jacob saw a ladder set up on earth and to the top of it reached Heaven: and behold the angels of God ascending and descending on it."*

One must know that you cannot tap into God. You must seek Him with your whole heart. Spirit speaks to spirit. Elohim seeks those that worship through His Holy Spirit and truth. You can draw from Him because He is the Well of Salvation. We go before His throne with boldness and confidence believing that He is a rewarder of those that diligently seek Him. To connect with the Heavenly Father, He invites us to develop a relationship with Him through His Son, the Lord and Savior Jesus Christ, through prayer and through worship. In the book of Revelation 3:20 we read, *"Behold, I stand at the door and knock: if any man hears my voice and open the door. I will come in to him and will sup with him, and he with me."* We find the invitation to come and sit with Jesus Christ and learn of Him. God is looking to establish a relationship with His people. He is looking to establish a relationship with you.

When an individual taps into the spirit, I believe he or she is tapping into the second realm; the realm of the occultic-spiritual, which is Satan's domain. Tapping opens the door to the demonic. An example will be a familiar spirit: you may dream of a deceased relative or friend visiting you in your dreams. You may assume that it's a sign from the heavens or from God, but that is far from the truth; it's a familiar spirit. There is a thin line between the supernatural and the occult-spiritual realm. One must be very careful when dealing with the spiritual world. We are admonished by the Word of God found in the book of 1 John 4:1 *"Beloved, believe not every spirit, but try the spirits whether they are of God"* because everything jumping and shouting, speaking in tongues may not be filled with God's Holy-Spirit; *"devils appear as angels of light"* (2 Corinthians 11:14).

How do you try the spirit to see whether it is of God or Satan? Become a fruit inspector, Galatians Chapter 5 clearly lists the fruit of the spirit and the works of the flesh. Galatians 5:19 *Now the works of the flesh are manifest, which are these: Adultery, fornication, uncleanness, lasciviousness. 20. Idolatry, witchcraft, hatred, variance, emulations, wrath, strife, seditions, heresies, 21. Envying, murders, drunkenness, reveling and such like of the which I tell you before as I have also told you in time past that they which do such things shall not inherit the kingdom of God.*

I implore you to examine yourself and make sure that you are not practicing or participating in the works of the flesh. Another way of trying the spirit is to watch how the individual treats or interacts with others. If they are prideful, always gossiping, hurling accusations, or looking for fault in someone, the red flags are waving.

If you are struggling with any fruit of the flesh, repent...ask God's Holy Spirit to help you do better, to be a better person, to fill you afresh, and surrender the throne of your heart to the Lord Christ Jesus.

■■

The fruit of the Spirit are listed as love, joy, peace longsuffering, gentleness, goodness, faith, meekness, temperance.

- ❖ Love – covers a multitude of sin. Love does not wish harm or ill-will towards any man.
- ❖ Joy – is a peaceful happiness not determined by circumstances.
- ❖ Peace – is a quietness, a not violent, serenity.
- ❖ Longsuffering – unlimited patience with understanding.
- ❖ Gentleness – not harsh, cautious
- ❖ Goodness – compassionate, caring
- ❖ Faith – hopeful, confidence in God, believing, trusting.
- ❖ Meekness – humility, respectful
- ❖ Temperance – level headed, not hasty, slow to speak, slow to anger.

People should be able to see the fruit of God's Holy Spirit emulating from you. Take notice of your behavior, your attitude towards others and self. Your fruit should reflect the characteristics of God. Produce good fruit.

CHAPTER 1

Normal Abnormalities

Normal abnormalities is a disclaimer; we all know that we are responsible for our actions. I want you the reader to understand/to see the difference between normal, natural abnormalities and the influence of the spiritual world. Just to name a few forms of normal abnormalities, they are: mental illness, learning disabilities, autism, OCD, anxiety disorders, dissociate disorders, Emotional disorders, pervasive development disorders, ADHD, and disruptive behavioral.

We understand that these abnormalities are natural; during the pregnancy, the brain, the nervous system, the DNA strands, or a body part (s) did not develop properly. However, with today's technology, science and education, services are available to help individuals. Nor are we referring to a strong personality. After a while (hopefully), the individual will realize a change for the better is needed, and healing, deliverance, a new way of thinking, and/or new habits will form because of your relationship with Christ or because you just want to do right.

Now we can look at the spiritual aspect of things. God has given us a special gift called "discernment." Discernment is having spiritual insight to see the motives of an individual's intentions or to identify the spiritual aspect of a thing. The gift of discernment helps us to distinguish who/what is of God and who/what is not of God. I experience the gift of DISCERNMENT in three ways, and others may as well. Sometimes I can look at a person and their countenance will be either light or dark. If their demeanor is dark, it could mean three things: 1. Oppression, 2. an unhuman characteristic in their facial feature which will be confirmed by their behavior, and 3. death.

There is a stark difference between a naturally being sad compared to a spiritual sadness. Naturally when a person experiences a moment of sadness, he or she will mope for a period, accept the outcome and move on. Spiritually, there is a heavy oppression that may be hard to shake loose; after fasting and prayer or seeking godly counsel, spiritual deliverance will take place. Another example of spiritual abnormalities is when you are applying biblical principles along with practical tools to your life step by step, you dot every I and cross every T, yet you still experience major setbacks and limitations.

Spiritual discernment is hearing and smelling as well. A good example of "smelling discernment" is, in the month of May 2018 during the prayer hour while at work in the school building, I began to smell the fragrance of Frankincense. A week later, after leaving church, about a quarter of a mile away from the church building, the aroma of Frankincense filled my car. After much research, I learned this experience was an indication of God receiving the prayers of His people, the prayers of the righteous.

My last example of spiritual discernment is the display of abnormal spiritual behavior. Suspicious behavior may be displayed in many forms. For example: the perpetrator will display the characteristic of being paranoid. Years ago, I was riding NJ Transit and a passenger who was a total stranger kept looking back at me. My stop came up. Yes, he got off at the same stop... anyways... as I was crossing the street, the young man stopped in the middle of the street and said, "WHY ARE YOU FOLLOWING ME!!!"

Just like everyone else I kept walking and made it to my destination safely. He displayed abnormal behavior of being paranoid; believe me, devils are disturbed by the presence of God. My last example of abnormal behavior is a perpetrator who watches every move you make – who you are talking to, where you parked your car, how you are dressed – they display an unnatural obsession with you. A good biblical example of abnormal spiritual behavior is found in the book of Acts, Chapter 16:16-18 "And it came to pass, as we went to prayer, a certain damsel possessed with a spirit of divination met us, which brought her masters much gain by soothsaying; 17 The same <u>followed</u> Paul and us, and cried, saying, These men are the servants of the most high God, which shew unto us the way of salvation. 18. <u>And this did she many days</u>, but Paul, being grieved, turned and said to the spirit, I command thee in the name of Jesus Christ to come out of her. And he came out the same hour."

Once again this is a great example of abnormal spiritual behavior. We must be watchful as well as prayerful. With God's Holy Spirit we should function in the same spiritual authority as Paul did.

As stated in the book of Acts 1:8 "ye shall receive power, after that the Holy Ghost is come upon you." You need God's Holy Spirit to deal with the spiritual/supernatural world.

Mark 16:17

And these signs shall follow them that believe: in my name shall they cast out devils; they shall speak with new tongues.

CHAPTER 2

The Things That God Hates

Can you imagine God hating something??? Well He does; there are certain things that He despises.

According to the Book of Proverbs 6:16-19 "Theses six things doth the Lord hate: yea, seven are an abomination unto him: 17. A proud look, a lying tongue, and hands that shed innocent blood. 18. A heart that devises wicked imaginations, feet that be swift in running to mischief. 19. A false witness that speakth lies, and he that soweth discord among brethren.

There are some other things that the Lord hates such as witchcraft, false prophets and the spirit of Jezebel. God hates witchcraft, the spirit of Jezebel, and false prophets because these practices cause God's people to go astray; to leave the truth of God by practicing idolatry and fornication. One must be mindful of this one purpose of idolatry and fornication, and that purpose is to replace the true living God. Every idol is a demonic host. Fornication is not only a physical act, it is an action that joins mind, body and soul together; the two become one. Your body is the temple of God, your body is God's physical house or body here on earth. Therefore, the Word of God states in 1 Corinthians "be ye not unequally yoked with unbelievers." We have all heard of the old adage "if you lay down with dogs, you'll get up with fleas." Be very prayerful and careful of those that you are associated with, especially those busybodies that are so anxious to get into your house/business. Everyone in the church does not have good intentions. Sometimes I wonder if he or she is truly a believer in Christ.

Scientifically a Macintosh apple seed will never produce a Sunkist orange and vice versa, a Sunkist Orange seed cannot produce a Macintosh apple; these fruits are distinctively different. Satan, witch-craft, false prophets, and the host of Jezebel cannot produce the fruit of God's Holy Spirit. Watch the fruit that people are producing.

Listen to what the Lord is saying to the church: In the Book of Revelation 2:20 "Notwithstanding I have a few things against thee, because thou suffer that woman Jezebel, which calleth herself a prophetess, to teach and to seduce my servants to commit fornication and to eat things sacrificed unto idols.

Ezekiel 13:1-2 "And the word of the Lord came unto me, saying Son of man, prophesy against the prophets of Israel that prophesy, and say thou unto them that prophesy out of their own hearts, Hear ye the word of the Lord; <u>Thus saith the Lord God; woe unto the foolish prophets, that follow their own spirit, and have seen nothing!</u>'

Whoa!!!! Somebody is in trouble!!!

Stay away from lying on God. If He spoke something to you, He will confirm His word and His will. You won't have to lie, steal, manipulate, intimidate or murder to get what the Lord has for you. Stay away from divination: horoscopes, astrology, psychics, palm reading, tea leaf reading, black magic: burning candles with spells and enchantments, and voodoo: potions, roots, blood sacrifices, Ouija boards, and séances; Stay away from these things.

Those that are professing Jesus Christ as their Lord and Savior should not be partakers of such acts.

Keep in mind "it is not God's will for man to die and go to Hell; it is His will for all to be saved, to be engrafted into His family through the Lord and Savior Jesus Christ." It is His will for your name and my name to be written in the Lamb's Book of Life. It is His will that you and I be filled with His Holy Spirit. It was never God's intention for you to be separated from Him. It was always

His intention for you and Him, and Him and I to be one.

John 3:16

"For God so loved the world that he gave his only begotten son, that whosoever believeth in him shall not perish but shall have everlasting life."

John 3:8

"For this purpose, the Son of God was manifested, that he might destroy the works of the devil."

CHAPTER 3

The Spirit of Jezebel

The Jezebel spirit has been around for ages. Historically, Jezebel was a Phoenician princess in the 9th century who married king Ahab. Historians noted that Jezebel's father, King Ethbaal, was a high priest of Astare, the Phoenician goddess. As the King's daughter, Jezebel served as a priestess to the idols, and she served the idol God Baal.

For political purposes, King Ahab of Israel married Jezebel the daughter of King Ethbaal of the land of Tyre. Despite her marriage to King Ahab, she refused to accept the God of Israel, Yahweh, as her God; instead King Ahab accepted the god Baal and erected an altar to the god Baal in the center of the city Samaria. This defiant act of King Ahab grieved the prophets and people of Israel. Historical facts tell us that Jezebel slaughtered the prophets of God and those that opposed her views. Ahab did not honor the commandments of God; Exodus 20:3-5: 3 Thou shalt have no other god before me. 4 Thou shalt not make unto thee any graven images, or any likeness of anything that is in heaven about, or that is in the earth beneath, or that is in the water under the earth. 5 Thou shalt not bow down thyself to them, nor serve them; for I the Lord thy God am a jealous God, visiting the iniquity of the fathers upon the children unto the third and fourth generation of them that hate me. Jezebel's defiant act of rejecting the God of Israel, caused the judgement of God to fall upon her and her household. The erecting of the altar of Baal caused King Ahab spiritually to mislead the Israelites by the way of idolatry. Idolatry causes one to make something else or someone else their god.

The spirit of Jezebel still functions in men and women the same today; controlling and manipulative. The spirit of Jezebel has two main objectives: the first objective is to dominate and control. This is done through the means of seduction, intimidation, fear, manipulation and witchcraft. He or she (the person the spirit of Jezebel is operating through) influences the leader through deception.

In a religious setting – the church, Jezebel seeks weak leadership. If the Pastor or Spiritual Leader is passive, weak minded or is more about themselves instead of God's will, the spirit of Jezebel host knows what to say, when to say it, how to dress, and most importantly, how to gain the trust of the Pastor. You must understand the enemy studies you. He or she makes it their business to know your likes and dislikes. This individual appears to be an angel of light; yet they assassinate the true prophets, and create a hostile environment through discord, strife, confusion and deception.

The consequences of tolerating a Jezebel spirit in the church can be detrimental. Lives will be affected, and the church doors will close. Trust me; no one wants to sit in a dead church.

Let us look at the following examples: First example – A middle aged couple, well educated and ordained by God, whose ministry was devasted by the works of the Jezebel spirit; while going along with church as usual, the couple's ministry was destroyed from the inside out by someone they knew and trusted. Unfortunately, this individual had alternative motives. What once was a full house -- a thriving house – soon emptied within a matter of time. The Pastor and his wife did everything they could to revive, to strengthen the house of God, to maintain what they had. Unfortunately, the hearts of the people were turned away. Despite the closing of the church doors, opportunities became available for the couple to continue to minister to the body of Christ.

A second example of the Jezebel spirit was the closing of an urban outreach ministry whose doors closed due to strife, confusion and so much more. The Deacons were fighting against the Pastor...Please make note: the primary function of a DEACON is to support the Pastor, help make the Pastor's load lighter. The Deacon's authority comes from the Pastor. The Pastor should not be intimidated or controlled by the DEACON BOARD.

The spirit of Jezebel's main objective is to prevent the truth of God from going forward, a watered-down, false gospel is being taught. A contaminated anointing is flowing. People are jumping and shouting, but no one is being healed, devils are not cast out, and deliverance is not taking place. When this happens, you're just going through the motions.

With church as usual, if traditional practices are rehearsed, the spirit of Jezebel is not easily identifiable. It is Satan's goal to keep the church in a carnal state with a watered-down gospel. When the Kingdom of God manifests in the house of God, the spirit of Jezebel shows itself through disruptive behavior such as jealousy, strife, confusion/discord, manipulation and intimidation. That spirit literally fights against worship and the true prophetic. For example, he or she will criticize the worship or service of others; you must know everyone cannot enter the presence of God. Everyone does not have an audience with the Lord. I believe it is a condition of the heart, that will allow an individual to freely give unto the Lord.

The second goal of the Jezebel spirit is to mislead the people of God by combining traditional religious practices with witchcraft or placing a greater emphasis on works and programs then on God Yahweh. We do a lot of things to build the church community. Be very careful when doing so. Everything that looks good is not a good thing for the house of God (The House of God is not an entertainment center). A good example of the Jezebel spirit manifesting in the church is the attempt to stop the true prophetic flow of God's Holy Spirit. A fire storm of lies and accusation attempts to destroy the works of God but... When the worship of the Lord's people is acceptable and pleasing unto him, the Lord Jehovah opens the windows of Heaven and pour out a blessing that we do not have enough room to receive. He fills the house with His glory. Souls are saved, broken hearts are mended, and the captives are set free. The man or woman of God functions on a whole new level; that apostolic/prophetic flow floods the house of God; God is glorified.

I've also witnessed an individual forming a group of people to fast and pray for the failure and demise of an individual(s) in the church. The witch will target an individual in their prayers which is accompanied with the burning of candles which is a form of Black Magic. They also use intimidation and manipulation to gain control of the house of God. That Jezebel spirit is very territorial. The spirit of Jezebel hates the presence of God. During the worship experience, he or she is sort of like a fish out of the water; they cannot function in the presence of God, so they will attempt to minimize the importance of worship, minimize the importance of praise, and minimize the importance of prayer; he or she functions heavily in jealousy. As long as he or she keeps the atmosphere carnal with discord and confusion, they have done their job.

The Jezebel spirit has a need for devoted eunuchs or servants. These individuals are Jezebel's eyes and ears (spies). They watch and repeat word for word what is being said or done. The eunuch seeks Jezebels approval whatever she/he says, they do. One of the greatest tools used by the Jezebel host is control and manipulation; The Jezebel host dominates through isolation and the manipulation of emotions of an individual. Oftentimes, the individual is in the state of uncertainty and fear; he or she is paranoid.

The Jezebel spirit uses people as a tool to do its' bidding. This spirit will show up at your workplace, school, home, the family reunion; where ever people are, the devil, the accuser, the opposer always shows up. The eunuchs, the puppets of Jezebel usually function in a state of confusion He or she knows what is going on is wrong, yet they continue to follow through with their actions in fear of retaliation from the Jezebel host. This is more than a person with a strong personality or who is insanely jealous, this is demonic. The host of the Jezebel spirit uses the following weapons to accomplish his or her goals.

- **Seduction** – is the process of deliberately enticing a person to engage in relationship, to lead astray as from duty, rectitude or the like, to corrupt to persuade or induce to engage in sexual behavior. I once heard "the devil will never tempt you with what you do not like."
- **Intimidation** – frighten or over awe (someone) specially to make them do what one wants.
- **Manipulation** – control or influence a person or situation cleverly, unfairly or

unscrupulously. To manage or influence skillfully especially in an unfair manner: to manipulate people's feelings, using people to carry out one's agenda.
- **Fear** – An unpleasant emotion caused by the belief that someone or something is dangerous likely to cause pain or a threat.
- **Witchcraft** – The practice of magic sorcery especially black magic, the use of spells and the invocations of spirits. Communication with the devil or familiar spirits, an irresistible influence or fascination.
- **Black magic** – involving the supposed invocation of evil spirits for evil purposes.
- **Jealousy** is a wicked device; the individual that is harboring jealousy hates without a cause. For some apparent reason he or she believes that you do not deserve or do not qualify for the blessings of the Lord; they literally covet you.
- **Slander/False Accusation** – the works of gossip is to discredit, to kill the reputation of someone else, to cause denial, disappointments and rejection.
- **Perversion** not only deals with sexuality; Perversion is the distorting of truth, changing the natural form of something for an unclean use. Once again, the objective

of the spirit of Jezebel is to prevent the truth of God from going forward which will cause the people of God to go astray.

The Tactics of Jezebel
If an individual refuses to submit to the act of intimidation, the host of Jezebel will use slander to cause harm to the person's reputation... the spread of lies and rumors to distort the perception of others. Slander is like venom that seeps into the ear gates which contaminates one's judgement.

The spirit of Jezebel will always cause one to second guess the Word of God (God is not the author of confusion). We are all aware of the prime example found in the book of Genesis where the "serpent beguiled Eve." Eve questioned God's authority regarding eating the fruit from the Tree of Knowledge. Did God really mean what He said??? Will we truly die if we eat of the fruit???

Also, we find in the book of Galatians 3:1 where Paul asked the question "Who bewitched you?" who caused you to stray away from the truth? Who?? Who caused you to disobey God??

The Jezebel spirit also targets families. Marriage and Family was the first institution that the Lord Jehovah established here on earth.

Marriage and family reflect God and the church. Marriage and family serve the purpose of God. Marriage represents the relationship of Jesus Christ and the Church. The Jezebel Spirit is that strange woman or man that comes to destroy families through adultery and misfortunes. The dysfunctions of an individual's hurts and wounds are doorways that this wicked spirit will use to gain control of an individual's fears and lack of understanding to discredit the purpose of marriage and family.

Prayer

Father God, in the name of Jesus, I thank you for allowing me to come before you this hour; I thank you, Father God, that you are not limited by time or place; You are the Great Jehovah. No one or thing can compare to you. You are Holy, you are just, righteous, and magnificent; you are Elohim. Father God, I thank you for being my present help in trouble times, times of trouble. You are my shield and rear guard; you are the rock that I am hewn from.

I have no reason to fear. I will not fret myself because of evildoers, neither will I be envious against the workers of iniquity; for vengeances is yours.

Father God, just like you anointed and appointed Jehu to destroy the wicked woman Jezebel, thank you for your anointing to do the same today. Therefore, in the name of Jesus Christ, I destroy the yokes of bondage: manipulation, intimidation and fear. Satan, you have no authority over the people of God, and no authority in the House of God. No longer will you wreak havoc in the lives of God's people. No longer will you destroy families.

By the power of Jesus Christ, I bind the spirit of Jezebel, her children and servants and cast them into outer darkness. In the name of Jesus Christ, I release the consuming fire of God upon the works of strife, discord, jealousy, malice, deception, depression, suicide and accusation.

Father God in the Mighty name of Jesus Christ, I break the curse of ACCUSATION, every lie that has been spoken to discredit the people of God, to cause denial, to cause betrayal and disappointments, I break right now in the name of Jesus Christ. Every lie that has been spoken to cause confusion, strife and discord, I cast down these wicked imaginations and these wicked words in the mighty name of Jesus Christ.

In the name of Jesus Christ, every word that witch spoke, every word that warlock spoke, every work of black magic, white magic, voodoo, hex/spell, and enchantment I send back to the house of those witches and warlocks in the mighty name of Jesus Christ. Cause them to fall into their own snare, their own trap. Your Word says Lord God, no weapon formed shall prosper against your child; no weapon formed will prosper. In the mighty name of Jesus AMEN! AMEN! AMEN!

Second Timothy 1:7

For God hath not given us the spirit of fear; but of power, and of love, and of a sound mind.

CHAPTER 4

Spiritual Wives and Spiritual Husbands

For lack of understanding the issue of "spiritual husbands and spiritual wives is a very complex topic that Christians rarely talk about. "The spiritual husband and spiritual wife are specially commissioned by Satan to molest, trouble and scatter good and godly homes, relationships and lives in general." *(Sam Udoubak July 2, 2015)*

The spiritual wives are identified by the name Succubus. The spiritual husband is identified by the name Incubus.

Spiritual wives and spiritual husbands are associated with night terrors, and demonic visitation. Usually the victim or prey experiences sexual encounters during their sleep or in the form of masturbation or pornography. These spirits attach themselves through the eye gate, ear gate, and dreams or they are transferred from one person to another. There is also a possibility, because of a hurtful experience, that one will accept the ungodly union made through deception.

A soul tie can develop through sexual or emotional activities. This is done by the releasing or distributing oneself in the form of DNA, intellectual or spiritual deposits. The wrong soul tie can bind an individual in an ungodly relationship. The Bible states in the book of 1 Corinthians 6:15-20 "What? Know ye not that he which is joined to a harlot is one body." The key word here is joined. Who did you connect with? Who did you give yourself to? Who are you having trouble letting go of or getting over??? For example: a marriage can be troubled by memories of a former companion you dated 20 years ago… Also 2 Corinthians 6:14-17 implores us Christians to "Be ye not unequally yoked with an unbeliever. What fellowship does light have with darkness?" Just to add, just because he or she is a Christian does not mean you are equally yoked; establishing a relationship is more than physical attraction. Does the individual compliment you/add to your life in a positive sense or does he or she deplete you or frustrate your life?

Sometimes out of loneliness one will connect or establish a relationship out of fear of being alone. Some may connect with individuals because of appearance and tolerate the unspeakable.

Some connect with individuals because he or she strokes the ego or whispers enticing words in the ears; many minister's marriages were destroyed because of what was or is appealing to the eye, to the flesh. We find this to be true in the story of Samson and Delilah found in the Book of Judges 16:4. Despite the many pleadings from his parents, Samson was determined to have things his way. Delilah was appealing to Samson's eyes. She spoke enticing words in his ears. She stroked his ego, and she won his trust. Delilah turned out to be the death of him.

In spite of, these wicked spirits are no match for the power of God. As a believer in Christ Jesus, you have the authority to break free from spiritual bondage and to live in the liberty provided by our Lord, Jesus Christ. You have the right to divorce yourself from these demonic spirits. You have the right to sever the soul ties with individuals that are not good for you. And this can be done through the power of God's Holy Spirit. I am stressing the point that you have to want to be free. Once God delivers you, don't go back.

Prayer of Renunciation

Father God, in the Name of Jesus, I am asking for forgiveness for all my sins and iniquities, create in me a clean heart and renew a right spirit within me. Forgive me for tolerating demonic forces and the influences that it has had upon my life.

In the Name of Jesus Christ, I renounce, I divorce the spiritual wife Succubus and the spiritual husband Incubus. In the Name of Jesus Christ, I renounce every ungodly soul tie.

In the Name of Jesus, I renounce lust of the eye and the flesh. I renounce the spirit of perversion; Cleanse me Lord Jesus, fill me with your Holy Spirit. I give you every hurt, every pain of rejection, abandonment, fear, bitterness and unbelief.

In the Name of Jesus, I renounce pride and every self-imposed curse. I humble myself before you; I surrender the throne of my heart to you Jesus Christ; be my Lord and Savior.

Thank you, Father God for destroying the yokes of bondage and for destroying strongholds. I thank you for the strength to turn away from those individuals and situations that are not healthy and beneficial to me. Thank you, Father God for the new thing that you are doing in me, replenishing me, rebuilding me, and restoring me.

I am a new creature in you, no longer bound by my past, no longer bound by fear. Thank you for perfecting those things that concern me. Thank you for strengthening me in my inner man in the might of your power. In the Name of Jesus, I am free. In the Name of Jesus, I am delivered. In the name of Jesus, I am healed, AMEN. AMEN. AMEN.

CHAPTER 5

Strongholds

A spiritual stronghold is a lie which we have allowed to distort or confuse our thinking; a lie can gain a foothold within our mind, emotions and then behavior. If we allow a lie to reside within, then that lie, like a seed, will produce its fruit which will distort the way we see and think. Because every lie is rooted in darkness, the fruit of every lie will eventually reflect the nature of darkness.

One can overcome a spiritual stronghold by accepting and believing the truth. What is truth?? Truth is "most often used to mean being in accord with fact or reality," also sincerity, candor, authenticity. The Word of God is truth. This is an absolute fact. God is not a liar; example – lie: God does not care about humanity; the truth: God so loved the world that He gave His only begotten son Jesus Christ, that whosoever believes in Him (Jesus Christ) shall not perish but have everlasting life. Another example of truth is "oil and water do not mix; this is a scientific fact. Try this experiment at home. The supplies that you will need are: one glass, 1 cup of oil (cooking oil or baby oil it does not matter) and 1 cup of water. Pour the 1 cup of oil, then the 1 cup of water into the same glass, and watch the truth develop before your eyes.

Knowing the truth will determine how you will perceive or view an issue. Light is synonymous to truth. Light expels darkness. Truth dispels lies. Sometimes the truth can be harsh/candid. Despite your feelings, you accept the truth, resolve the issue within yourself and move on.

Unfortunately, everyone does not like the truth. He or she will believe a lie if it is beneficial to them despite the consequences. Confessing the Word of God, praying, speaking truth to truth over your circumstances, and living by faith as you implement practical methods such as, taking ownership of your actions, taking the necessary steps to make corrections, and seeking godly professional counseling/therapy destroys strongholds.

- instead of saying "I can't" confess "I can do all things through Christ who strengthens me." Keep trying until you accomplish your goal.

- Instead of focusing on the dark clouds, keep in mind that the sun is always shining.

- Instead of believing that you are always right, take a deep breath, sit down and talk with someone that is a bit wiser, and more experienced than you are.

The Word of God states in Proverb 3:5-6 "Trust in the Lord with all thine heart and lean not unto thy own understanding; acknowledge him in all thy ways and he will direct thy path." Also, in the Book of James Chapter 1 verse 5 it is stated "If any of you lack wisdom let him ask of God, that giveth to all men liberally and upbraideth not; and it shall be given him."

God will never leave us to fend for ourselves; the truth will always prevail.

Prayer

Father God in the name of Jesus Christ, I thank you for creating me in your image. Father, I ask for you to create in me a clean heart and fill me afresh with your Holy Spirit. I thank you Father God, that my mind is renewed after the Spirit of your Word. I thank you Lord God, for enlightening the eyes of my understanding so that can I make sound decisions and healthy and wise choices.

Therefore, in the name of Jesus Christ I tear down every stronghold: lies, other people's opinions, discouragements erroneous philosophies, theories, assumptions, concepts, beliefs, and negative thoughts that have been built up over the years. I cast down these wicked imaginations, in the Name of Jesus.

I thank you Father God, for a peaceful mind. As I meditate on your Word and good thoughts, I am filled with your peace. I hide your Holy Word in my heart, and I remember your testimonies which cause me to hope.

In Jesus' name I pray AMEN! AMEN! AMEN!

Numbers 23:23

"Surely there is no enchantment against Jacob, neither is there any divination against Israel: according to this time it shall be said of Jacob and of Israel, What hath God wrought?"

CHAPTER 6

Witchcraft

Witchcraft in its simplest form is rebellion against God's authority. Stubbornness is disobedience to God's will. Example: I'll do it my way when I get ready to. Other forms of witchcraft are intimidation, manipulation and dominance. The objective of witchcraft is total control or destruction of a person's life or the church. If you have encountered intimidation, manipulation and dominance in the church, know without a doubt you are dealing with the spirit of witchcraft. Something is not right when a person uses illegal demonic powers to gain control of an individual or the people of God.

Bishop Nicholas Duncan-Williams said it beautifully in his message: The Ongoing War. "The problem with the church today, we don't call things by its name anymore. The reason why things are not changing in our lives is because we are polishing it up; you cannot counsel demons."

Absolutely…because ministers choose to counsel demons instead of using their <u>spiritual authority</u> and casting them out, deliverance does not take place. Instead you are just going through the motions.

- Today's witches in the church practice black magic, enchantments, divination, works of voodoo, and sanitaria.
- What people fail to realize is spiritual warfare is real and you cannot intellectualize it. It takes a revelation from God, His strategies, and His power to defeat the demonic forces. You cannot rationalize this. Yahweh is very specific about the structure of the church and the order of doing things. King Saul is a great example of a minister who compromised with witchcraft. In the book of 1 Samuel, Chapter 28 beginning with verse 6 the Lord God discontinued communication with Saul; not a word, not a dream. It's a terrible thing to be separated from God. King Saul did not repent. Instead he continued with his behavior and sought guidance from another source.

As a minister of God, if you find yourself in the position of King Saul, repent of your sin and seek

God with your whole heart. Let's see what the Word of God says about repenting:

- Proverbs 28:13 He that covers his sins shall not prosper but whoso confesses and forsakes them shall have mercy."
- 1 John 1:9 If we confess our sins, he is faithful and just to forgive us our sins, and to cleanse us from all unrighteousness.
- Romans 10:9-10 That if thou shall confess with thy mouth the Lord Jesus and shall believe in thine heart that God hath raised him from the dead, thou shalt be saved. 10. for with the heart man believeth unto righteousness and with the mouth confession is made unto salvation.

Today, be honest with the Lord Jesus Christ, today accept Him as your Savior. Today repent of your sins.

The most common works of witchcraft that I witnessed taking place in the church are: black magic/divination, enchantment spells, curses and seduction.

Enchantment allows the witch or warlock to use an individual as a host to carry out their bidding...the host has a lack of control of his or her actions at that time because their mental or emotional state is not sound. The false becomes truth, what is not real seems real; it sounds right but something is off. There is a state of confusion.

The spirit of seduction uses spells, is very flirtish to make its host most desirable or irresistible. This practice creates within its victim an indecisive attitude, he or she becomes critical of every little thing, they become fault finders in others. No matter what you do or say, you would never be able to please him or her because the seductress seems to be what he or she wants.

Mind control is another tool of witchery. The witch/warlock insists, pressures you to do things their way, they use your words to bind you; even though you know it is wrong, you will act to fulfill the warlock's or the witch's commands. The witch or warlock will also use false accusations and threats such as God is going to punish you, if you refuse to comply.

Accusation the purpose of accusation is to discredit the character of an individual, to cause disappointments, denial and betrayal.

Other weapons that the witch and warlock will use are confusion, lying, and gossip to attack its target, the purpose for this verbal attack is to cause others to see things or the person through his or her eyes, to make its victim an outcast. Anything that goes wrong, the finger is pointed at the victim.

My personal experience in the church occurred when a member attacked my worship and prayer habits. This woman made it her business to pick at everything I did, from the way I greeted people to the style of shoes that I wore; she outright hated me. It got to the point that she convinced other women in the church to gather in prayer against me. That is a classic element of witchcraft; gathering in groups to pray against people for their hurt and demise. Jealousy and envy are open doors for Satan to enter a believer's/churchgoer's heart. Satan only needs one person to do his bidding, to cause confusion and strife in the House of God. Another account of witchcraft is when the enemy goes deep sea diving into your past and gathering information that he or she can use against you. He or she must find a reason to disqualify you from your present or future blessing. But God...our Heavenly Father, the Lord Jesus Christ forgave our sins and He cast the sins into the sea of forgetfulness. Who or what gives a person the right to go back 20 years, 30 years in a person's life for information to prevent them from moving forward? That is not the Spirit of God. That is the spirit of Satan. Do you see it? The spirit of witchcraft is a destructive tool of Satan.

One can identify the attack of witchcraft by the following experiences:

- Financial famine, constant denial,
- discord/the destruction of a family/marriage,
- repeated cycles, sort of like you are going in circles or wandering, unexplainable sickness, lack of sleep, being paranoid/fearful,
- unexplainable hinderances, regression instead of progression,
- depression, oppression, constantly frustrated, aggravated, vexed,
- isolation,
- turning away from the things of God, not praying, studying/devotional, not fasting,
- a state of fogginess, indecisiveness, not sober minded or unbelief just to name a few.

There were plenty of nights when apparitions and dark images appeared in my home. There were plenty of nights when a strong presence entered my room. On a few occasions, there was an impression on my bed as if a physical body was sitting in that very spot, along with tapping on the bed. My dreams were invaded by the witch through astral projection and sleep paralysis.

Thank God for the intercessory prayers of Prophet Vincent K. Kopod. Midnight prayers carried me through. Not only did the prayers carry me through; but my personal prayer life changed for the better. I began to grow as an intercessor, and as a believer in Christ Jesus.

Prophet Brian Carn's ministry *Encounters* provided strength to fast and pray along with better understanding of the various forms of witchcraft.

Bishop George Bloomer's ministry *Spiritual Authority* gave me the courage to stand and face my enemies in the religious setting. There are many religious institutions but very few Houses of God. These individuals' ministries answered questions and explained what I was dealing with and explained how to overcome the witchcraft. The pastor that I was under (at the time) was not in place to provide an explanation on how to overcome witchcraft or how to effectively conduct spiritual warfare. He was not in his proper place of authority to stop the enemy.

The Blood of Jesus! Because of the Blood of Jesus Christ, my enemies did not triumph over me.

*One must understand that Satan looks for an open door to gain access to the heart of man. A door can be: bitterness and rebellion, jealousy, rejection, lust, low self-esteem, unbelief, or pride. Any area in your life unsubmitted to God's Holy Spirit can become an open door for demonic spirits to influence a believer. Yes, it is true that the enemy can only suggest; if an individual entertains those thoughts, that seed of darkness will take root and grow. Unless he or she takes charge of those dark thoughts by bringing them into subjection and casting down wicked imaginations, those thoughts will take root and begin to produce.

Trust me any time an individual(s) can cause a distraction in the service to hinder the move of God, they are not governed by God's Holy Spirit. Anytime a person makes threats, uses slander spells/enchantments, to manipulate and control, that person is not governed by God's Holy Spirit. Anytime an individual can convince a person not to follow God's instruction or ways, that person is not governed by God's Holy Spirit. Anytime an individual in the church uses intimidation, manipulation and dominance, that person is operating in the spirit of witchcraft.

Prayer

If you find yourself dealing with Witchcraft pray this prayer:

Father God, I thank you for the authority and power that you have given me over Satan and the works of witchcraft. In the Name of Jesus Christ, I call for the fire of God to fall upon and consume the works of witchcraft, the works of black magic and the works of voodoo. In the mighty name of Jesus Christ, I cancel and make null and void every word curse that has been spoken against my life, my family, my health and my finances. I will not die but live and declare the works of the Lord. The works of my hands will prosper. I will enjoy the fruit of my labor. My mind is sober. I make sound and wise decisions. I do not have a spirit of fear but of power, love and a sound mind. I am a joint heir with Christ Jesus. The blessing of Abraham rests upon my household. Wealth and riches dwell in my household. My children and their children's children are blessed in the Name of Jesus Christ. We can not be cursed. For my righteousness goes before us. We can not be cursed for the angels of the Lord have been given charge over us. Our footsteps have been laid by the Lord Himself. Therefore in the name of Jesus

Christ I am blessed in every area of my life, in Jesus' name.

AMEN! AMEN! AMEN!

CHAPTER 7

Spiritual Authority

The weapons of our warfare are not carnal but mighty through the pulling down of every stronghold and the casting down of every wicked imagination.

Through God's Holy Spirit and through His Word, He has given us the power and authority to overcome, defeat, and conquer principalities, demonic influences, and curses. He has given us the power and authority to build, multiply, and to be fruitful. One must take to heart that the Lord watches over His Word to perform it. The job of His Word is to produce, to bring forth His will, to cause His kingdom to manifest as heaven on earth. Yes, He needs your mouth, your mind, and your hands. He needs you to show Himself strong here on earth.

It is of great importance that you are filled with God's Holy Spirit. The Word of God, in the book of Romans Chapter 8 stresses the importance of being filled with God's Holy Spirit specifically the following verses state: 15 but ye have received the Spirit of adoption, whereby we cry, Abba, Father. 16 The Spirit itself beareth witness with our spirit, that we are the children of God. 17 And if children, then heirs; heirs of God, and joint-heirs with Christ.

Besides sonship, God's Holy Spirit intercedes for us; He talks to the Lord on our behalf. 26 Likewise the Spirit also helpeth our infirmities: for we know not what we should pray for as we ought: but the Spirit itself maketh intercession for us with groanings which cannot be uttered. 27 And he that searcheth the hearts knoweth what is the mind of the Spirit, because he maketh intercession for the saints according to the will of God.

If it was not for the Holy Spirit where would I be??? There were plenty of times I sat at the altar not knowing what to say or how to pray – but God... His Holy Spirit interceded for me, His prayers covered me in unknown areas, His prayers uprooted and put a stop to the plans of the enemy. Because the Holy Spirit interceded for me, my mind is sound. Because of God's Holy Spirit, my family is safe and sound. Because of God's Holy Spirit, I am more than a conqueror. I am an overcomer because of God's Holy Spirit.

Prayer

Father God, I accept Jesus Christ as my Lord and Savior. I ask in the name of Jesus Christ that you fill me with your Holy Spirit with the evidence of speaking in tongues. Create in me a clean heart, renew in me a right spirit. Cause my mind to be renewed after the spirit of your word. I surrender the throne of my heart to you. I surrender those secret places to you. On this day Father God, seal me with your Holy Spirit.

In your matchless name Jesus Christ, I pray. AMEN! AMEN! AMEN!

Psalms 18:34

He teaches my hands to war, so that a bow of steel is broken by mine arms.

CHAPTER 8

Weapons of Warfare

The weapons of our warfare are as follows:

- Praise
- Worship
- Prayer
- The Word of God
- The armor of God which consist of:
- The Helmet of Salvation
- The Breastplate of Righteousness
- The Belt of Truth
- The Preparation of the Gospel
- The Shield of Faith
- The Sword of the Spirit
- The Blood of Jesus

1. "Praise with the clapping of hands," Psalm 140 (144?) "The Lord teaches our hands to

war." The clapping of hands creates a sound of confusion in the ears of the enemy.

- ❖ Praising God with a song and a dance defeats discouragement and fear.
- ❖ Singing praises causes an individual to be empowered with the might of God.
- ❖ Praising God causes the earth to bring forth its fruits (causes prosperity to come forth in your life).
- ❖ Praising God releases your situation into the hands of God.
- ❖ God inhabits, dwells, lives in the praises of His people.
- ❖ Your praise is an acceptable and pleasing sacrifice unto God.

I implore you today to praise God especially when you don't feel up to it. Give God praise. If you only knew how powerful your praise is, you will...PRAISE GOD!!!

- Your praise will cause doors to open.
- Your praise will cause shackles to be broken.
- Your praise will cause a shifting to take place in your life. It provides a place for the Lord to abide, to dwell in.
- Your praise is full of power; it is powerful.

2. Worship is an intimate, a private, and an unveiling moment with God. A few biblical moments of intimacy with God are as follows: God and Abraham because of their relationship (take a moment and listen to their conversations), Abram and the Lord Jehovah became friends; Imagine that your devotional time with the Lord Jesus Christ will help foster a close relationship with the Lord. Another example of biblical worship is: King David; his worship caused him to grow; it caused him to mature to become a man after God's own heart. His worship transitioned him from the field to the palace. I have learned over the years that an individual's worship must be authentic. It must come from the heart. Worship stirs the heart of God, it causes Him to come to see about you. Your worship ushers in the glory of God; the heavens open. Your worship incapacitates the enemy. In the corporate setting of the church, worship causes the Apostolic/Prophetic anointing to flow; the sick are healed, yokes are broken, the captives are set free, devils are cast out, no one leaves the same. A new experience... a God encounter.

I dare you to worship God. Open your heart and commune with Him, give Him your best, be honest with the Lord and watch what He does. My God. Watch what He will do!!! He will move the heavens for you. Everyone, I mean everyone will stand in awe, when the Living God shows up on your behalf and defends you. I implore you to worship the Lord in the beauty of holiness; give Him what He requires.

3. Prayer-Christ has given us the authority to bind and to loose, to proclaim, to decree and to declare. Christ has given us the liberty to call upon His name; He welcomes our fellowship, He looks forward to spending quality time with us.

Spiritual warfare really teaches you how to pray. You will learn to search the scriptures for the right words to pray. There are many prayers in the scriptures that we can adopt and apply to our circumstances. You can draw from the book of Psalms. You can draw from 1 Peter. One of the most famous prayers is Psalm 23:1 "The Lord is my shepherd I shall not want." In this verse we discovered the Lord is a provider and protector; you shall not lack. Example: I would pray accordingly; Thank you Father God for being my divine protection and provision. I thank you for causing the works of my hands to bring forth financial gain. I think you for divine connections and divine disconnection.

It's okay to pray. It's okay to pour your heart out to God. It's okay to be honest with the Lord. It is okay to pray.

One thing about prayer is you must do the footwork. You must participate and work smart to bring forth the results that you are believing the Lord for. Put your practical tools to use.

- ❖ Prayer of Intercession – when we the believer go before God in prayer on behalf of others. John 20:23 and Genesis 18:23-33

- ❖ Prayer of Supplication – we petition or plead humbly to God for a special need or desire. 1 Peter 5:7 and Matthew 11:28.

- ❖ Prayer of Thanksgiving – counting our blessings, naming them one by one. Appreciating God's goodness and mercies. Psalm 100:4-5

- ❖ Prayer of Spiritual Warfare – fighting against the enemy from a spiritual stance through prayer and fasting which will cause the victory to manifest in the natural. Psalms 18:34 and 2 Corinthians 10:4-6.

- ❖ Prayer of Communion – a time of worship and adoration; a time of you meditating on God's greatness; A time of honoring God for who he is. Matthew 6:9-14 and Psalms 103:1.

- ❖ Prayer of Tears – silent tears speak volumes of a heavy heart, Luke7:44-48 and Psalm 126.

- ❖ Prayer of Speaking In tongues – God's Holy spirit intercedes for us. He prays for those things that we do not know about or when we do not know how to pray for a circumstance Romans 8:27.

4. The Word – "Man shall not live by bread alone but by every word that proceeds out of the mouth of God" The Word of God has an assignment. Its' purpose is to manifest the will of God in the lives of His people. The Word of God is sharper than any two-edged sword; this two-edged sword cuts with precision separating the Holy from the unholy. The Word of God exceeds space and time, speak the Word of God over your circumstances. Confessing God's Word serves as a spiritual weaponry revealing His will, which reveals His character and His attributes. The Word of God is God Himself in the literal form. When we sit and read the scripture we are communing with

God. When we meditate on the Word of God, we are becoming as He is.

5. Love – the Love of God is amazing. Showing compassion to our fellow man is showing love to God. Through acts of kindness such as feeding the hungry and clothing the naked; when we are compassionate with our fellow man, we are lavishing God with love. "We cannot hate our brother or sister to the point of their destruction who we see; and love God who we do not see." Love does not permit jealousy or envy to function in its domain, 1 John. The Love of God is phenomenal. When we allow the love of God to flow through us, then we can love our enemies and pray for those that prosecute us and despitefully use us. The love of God is phenomenal; it does not wish or hope for evil.

6. The Helmet of Salvation protects our minds from confusion, erroneous information and philosophies. Sometimes we can find ourselves being bombarded with a million thoughts a minute. Sometimes the issues of life can become overwhelming with stress and fears. Stress and fears fight against our faith and beliefs. Learning to commit our thoughts unto the Lord Jesus brings us into a state of

peace This state of peace voids confusion within; we think clearly and make sound/good decisions.

Wearing the helmet of Salvation is wearing protective gear that provides coverage for one's belief and one's faith in God. It gives you a sturdy head in this life.

- "Let this mind be in you which was also in Christ Jesus."

7. The Breastplate of Righteousness – because of your relationship with the Lord Jesus Christ, you are in good standing with God the Father. Biblically speaking Aaron, the High Priest's breastplate was designed specifically by God to identify the twelve tribes of Israel with twelve stones. Each jewel was unique with the inscription of the names of the twelve tribes of Israel.

Your breastplate of righteousness is an indication of your belonging to the Tribe of Judah. Jesus Christ "Yeshua" is a descendant of the Tribe of Judah, He is referred to as "the Lion of Judah." Your breastplate of righteousness also represents the status or rank of your priesthood. You are just not any old priest. Your priesthood is linked to the kingship of the King of kings, your spiritual authority comes from King of kings for He sits in heavenly places, on the throne of righteousness.

Walk in the authority that Christ has given you.

8. The Belt of Truth gives you the spiritual support you need that holds the armor in place, sort of like a girdle or shapewear. The Belt of Truth requires that we are honest with ourselves and most importantly, that we are honest with the Lord. The belt of truth ensures full coverage, meaning all gaps are closed. The truth of God dispels darkness, and it defeats lies. To overcome the lies of the enemy, we need to accept the truth and apply God's truth to our life circumstances.

9. Your Feet – footwear is very important; wearing the improper shoe will cause damage to the foot, knees and back. The improper shoe will expose the feet to hidden dangers on the ground or under the ground. Improper footwear cannot provide enough protection for the various terrains and weather. Example: historically noted is the Confederate army lost the American Civil War because of lack of

resources and supplies; one supply that the troops had dire need of were boots/shoes. History tells us because of no shoes and lack of other supplies, the Confederate Army was at a great disadvantage and lost the war (which was a good thing).

Your footwear – the Gospel of Jesus Christ, the Word of God – will cause you to stand in adverse moments. It will provide enough protection and support in all types of trials and tribulations as you walk along this journey. As you are walking upon the scorpion and serpents, the Word of God divinely protects you from the enemy's bites and stings. Whatever challenges you are facing today, make sure the Word guides you through. Make sure the Word of God will cause you to stand before kings and walk amongst the great. The Word of God will cause you to travel the paths that God has ordained for you. Should you lack direction, "acknowledge the Lord in all thy ways and he will direct thy path." It is so easy to do this thing by yourself or travel other avenues for an answer or the truth, but when your feet are covered with the Gospel of Jesus Christ, you will walk in the footsteps that the Lord has prepared for you; you are walking in the right direction for your life.

10. The shield of faith is our confidence in God. The shield of faith protects you from the fiery darts of unbelief, confusion, lies, deceit, and the impossible. Whatever the enemy launches at you, your faith protects you.

Historically shields were made from various materials such as wood overlaid with leather and framed by bronze depending on the military style. For example, the Greeks used the designer of a Hoplon/aspis shield, this shield was round. The Romans' Parma shield was designed in the oblong shape made to cover the whole body. the Roman shield was redesigned for the purpose of distinguishing their military from the Greek military. They also mastered the formation styles (Phalanx) of shield usage from the Greeks.

The Normans' Shield was the Kite design. This design made it easy for the horsemen to carry, and it hung around the neck (sought of like a shoulder back or backpack) which offered better protection. As you can see every civilization's military developed a shield to protect its soldiers while in battle. Every training session taught the soldier how to use this device offensively and defensively.

This holds true with our shield of faith which we exercise during our trials and tribulation.

Each challenge teaches us to use our faith to overcome various obstacles. Each challenge teaches us to use our faith to accomplish great feats Our shield of faith helps protect our belief and our confidence in God.

11. The sword of the Spirit is the Word of God; It is our choice weapon. Every time the enemy says something, we respond with the Word of God. For example, the enemy says, "God does not love you." Your response will be "He will never leave me nor forsake me. He has loved me with an everlasting love." Speak the Word of God over yourself into your situations. Speak the Word of God to combat the attack of the enemy. Jesus Christ used His words to defeat Satan. For example, in the book of Matthew Chapter 4 verse 4 Jesus was tempted to turn the stone (s) into bread; Jesus combated the evil thought/wicked imagination with the Word of God. He stated, "It is written, Man shall not live by bread alone, but by every word that proceeds out of the mouth of God." Whatever the word of God says about your situation, state it, decree it, proclaim it, and release God into your situation. AMEN!!!

12. The Blood of Jesus Christ was shed for the remission of our sins. The blood of Jesus was shed for our healing. The Blood of Jesus was shed for our deliverance. When we plead the Blood of Jesus over our lives and over our families, we are applying divine protection to our households. All that applies to us is divinely protected because of the Blood of Jesus. The power of God's blood broke every curse. It breaks every act of witchcraft, black magic, voodoo, enchantment, and mind control. You must understand; when the crown of thorns was placed on Jesus' head, the blood flowed over His eyebrow - the curse of poverty was broken, droplets of His blood fell upon the earth- the curse of poverty was broken, believers would be no longer barren, no longer separated from God. When the Roman soldier pierced Jesus' side with his sword, they witnessed blood and water come forth to attest to the redemption of humanity. The blood of Jesus Christ broke the curse.

CHAPTER 9

Overcoming Witchcraft

I am triumphant. I wondered for some time, why me?? Why do I have to deal with the issue of witchcraft in the church? I always believed and knew the church to be a sacred place. A place to commune with God and a place to fellowship with like-minded believers. Certain things should not happen or be associated with the House of God. Unfortunately, they are. Unfortunately, witchcraft is still operating in some churches.

From my experience and what I have observed, if the leader is not mature or knowledgeable in the subject of spiritual warfare, he or she is most likely to fall prey or succumb to the influences of witchcraft. If the Pastor or Bishop associates themselves with individuals that are practicing witchcraft or functioning under the influence of the Jezebel spirit, he or she will compromise with that individual/that spirit. Once again if the pastor is under the wrong influence, the people will be under the wrong influence...the influence of witchcraft, a familiar spirit, the spirit of Jezebel will cause them to go astray.

We all know that God does not contradict Himself; He does not lie.

Being a part of a young thriving ministry things seemed to be normal, but things were not normal. Something was not quite right. I began experiencing demonic attacks. It seemed as though my world was falling apart. No matter how much I prayed and fasted, things seemed to get worse; instead of life becoming better, my world was turned upside down. I did not understand what was going on until I had an unsettling dream. I shared this dream with a friend of mine, in this dream "a woman turned towards me and opened her mouth. Bats began flying out of her mouth towards me." When I raised my hands to shield my face, I woke up. This dream troubled me for months with me not knowing this was a warning. Shortly after, other dreams followed. Dreams of pythons, one snake wrapped itself around the main beam of the church; which was an indication that the spirit of witchcraft had the leader in its' grip. Though the leader was able to deliver a mighty word and perform religious duties, they were still under the wrong spiritual influence. There were plenty of times that I sat in the sanctuary and saw an anaconda slither up the left aisle towards the pulpit.

One lesson that I've learned about ministry is the Lord God establishes each house with a unique purpose. I think it is sad that local ministers were not able to identify or pray me through. Some looked at me with unbelief and assumed that I was not telling the truth because of the magnitude of the ministry that I was associated with at the time. What was also striking was how they thought I could benefit their ministry during this time of my spiritual crisis. I'm not upset with them, I guess this was a learning experience for us all. Nevertheless, the Lord vindicated me in all cases.

In my book, *Healing of the Soul*, I mentioned in Chapter Three "Every time I walked away thinking it was the right thing to do; the Lord sent me back with no explanation." This time the Lord showed me somethings about me and about ministry. I had to learn to stand my ground and not run. You will never solve a problem by running away or pretending it does not exist. This holds true in every aspect of life. You must confront, own it, face it, deal with your issues. I dealt with this witchcraft issue in two ways: privately, I informed the Pastor. I asked the individual could we sit and talk about the issue in front of the mothers of the church, and she refused to do so. I handled the situation privately and discreetly. Members of the congregation did not know in detail what was going on. But God!!!! There were months of fasting and praying, months of being on the altar. In the month of August, the Lord, the Great Jehovah literally showed up in front of members and guests and revealed the truth and exposed the enemy. You cannot tell me that the Creator of the universe is not real. Officially released in God's timing, the Lord moved me to a better place – a safer place.

For weeks I struggled with the thought of "hiding in the cave." I refused to be like the prophet Elijah who ran to the cave to hide. I refused to suffer in silence. I refused to deal with this issue again. I refused to allow the enemy to get away with it; not this time. I opened my mouth and said something. I publicized it. Some people were shocked by my confession. Some were angered and spoke out of ignorance, and some stood up and apologized for the hurt that was caused. Because of the apologies and three good friends, I removed the post from my social media page. It took a while for the issue to simmer down and I tell you one thing, I do not have to deal with the issue of witchcraft any more from that person(s). I tell you, you must stand up for yourself. Do not allow people in the church and outside of the church to intimidate, manipulate, or dominate you. Do not allow individuals to tear down your character or crush your spirit or make you feel that you are less than. The same thing goes for the work place, that is why Human Resources exists. Make sure you document every event. Make sure you have a paper trail to cover yourself. You must protect yourself. You are not a verbal or physical punching bag; nor are you a doormat.

I witnessed the reality of God through this whole ordeal. God always vindicated me. He always shows up strong and mighty on my behalf. As I mentioned in a previous chapter, I believe every ministry has a specialty. I believe God's Holy Spirit will divinely connect you to individuals' ministries to perfect you and to cause you to mature in Christ Jesus. I have learned some great things from Apostle John Eckhardt and Apostle Ryan Le Strange; many, many, many questions were answered, and mine eyes of understanding were opened. I tell you the Lord does things in steps, step one, step two from glory to glory. "My time was not wasted." the truths that were revealed from the lessons that I have learned are precious treasures that cannot be discounted by the ignorance of others.

I worship, I praise God the way I do because He brought me out! He protected me. He caused the plan of the enemy to fail. I have a sound mind; my family is together, and we are safe.

Your private time with the Lord God is very important; you need that strength to endure hardness as a good soldier. Through your worship, the Lord God will download strategies; It does not matter what kind of spiritual battle you are fighting, get before God in prayer and fasting. For months, I went before the Lord on Saturday and Sunday mornings, I met him at the altar. There were plenty of times that I did not know what to pray or say, but I quietly positioned myself at the altar. Certain church folks talked about me and mocked me, but God...supernaturally provided for me, supernaturally protected me and my family.

I want you to be encouraged, empowered and liberated through the Word of God. I want you to be strengthened in your inner man in the might of God's power. I want you to take confidence in the fact that you are not alone nor, will you be made ashamed. "For thus saith the Lord fear thou not, I am with thee; be not dismayed for I am thy God: I will strengthen thee, yea I will help thee yea; I will uphold thee with the right hand of my righteousness. *Isaiah 41:10.* No weapon of witchcraft, jealousy, slander, or gossip formed against you will prosper. No weapon of black magic, Santeria, voodoo or any form of divination or enchantments will succeed against you. No weapon of poverty or limitations will prosper against you. You will not be a vagabond wandering here and there. You will not live beneath my means. You are a stable people, a thriving people, a prosperous people. You are a blessed people. For I cause my face to rise and shine upon you. I take delight, I rejoice in your prosperity. For I am your God and there is no other greater than "I AM."

Thus, saith the Lord.

CHAPTER 10

Break the Curse: Family

Prayer for Families:

Marriages: Father God in the name of Jesus Christ, we come before you on behalf of marriages. We thank you Lord God, for what you have joined together no man will put asunder/separate. We thank you Lord God for the marriage bed being undefiled. No weapon of adultery, of addiction, no weapon of strife, jealousy, no weapon of witchcraft will prosper against my marriage. Thank you for mending the broken heart, for mending the trust, the bond between husband and wife. Thank you for rekindling the passion and the hope for one another. Thank you, Lord God for my beloved husband, for his desire being for me. Thank you that I am set as a seal upon his heart. Thank you for protecting him, blessing the works of his hands. Cause him to prosper in every area of his life. Meet his deepest need, encourage him, empower him, liberate him.

Teach me Lord God, how to reverence him like I reverence you. Help me to be his support, especially when we do not see eye to eye.

Thank you, Father God, that I am my beloved's and my beloved is mine...in the name of Jesus Christ I pray... AMEN! AMEN! AMEN!

Families: Father God in the name of Jesus Christ we come before you on behalf of Families. We thank you for visiting every household. For meeting the needs of your people. Lord God, we lift the single parents; help Lord God. Be a present help and strength in the household. Encourage that mother. encourage that father as they do the best that they know how to provide and care for their children. Keep the children safe from every predator. Bless the children to enjoy the innocence of their youth. Bless every household with plenty of food. Thank you for every need being met. Thank you, Jehovah Raphia, for healing the hearts of the children that are dealing with rejection, abandonment and abuse. Place godly people in their lives to nurture them, to mentor them, to show them your love, that they may grow into well-rounded, healthy adults. Thank you for wrapping your loving arms of protection around every child; around every single parent.

Thank you for the blended families. Thank you for helping each family member to adjust to each other, to respect each other, to give each other a chance. To love each other. Thank you for helping and for teaching the mothers to be mothers. For helping and teaching the fathers to be fathers, grandparents to be grandparents, aunts and uncles to be aunts and uncles. Thank you for helping us to be whole not dysfunctional, to be loving and understanding, not bitter or resentful.

Thank you, Father God, for every single person who desires to marry and for those who do not desire marriage.

Thank you for helping us to be content in the state that we are in until you bring that man or that woman into our lives. Because it is not good for man to be alone. Thank you for the assurance that this is the person that you have ordained for my life. Out of all the examples set before us; we will customize our marriage to suit us, to glorify you. We are one as Christ is with the church.

For those who do not desire marriage, thank you for blessing their hearts with contentment, that their lives are used for your glory in the name of Jesus.

For those that are afraid to love again, thank you for healing the deep wounds, for setting them free from fear in the name of Jesus. At the right time Lord, bless them to love again.

Thank you, Lord God that many waters cannot quench love, neither can the floods drown it. In the name of Jesus Christ, we pray... AMEN! AMEN! AMEN!

Break the Curse: If you find yourself dealing with family issues, repeat this prayer: If need be you can alter this prayer to suit your situation.

Father God I come before you seeking forgiveness of all sins and iniquities committed by my ancestors ten generations back and more.

In the name of Jesus Christ, I break every ancestral curse that has been spoken against my family. I break every curse from <u>Mississippi</u>, <u>New Orleans</u> and <u>New Jersey</u>. Every demonic doorway, I command it closed and sealed by the power of the Holy Spirit. Every spirit that was released against my family and I, I bind in the name of Jesus Christ. I bind the strongman of oppression; I destroy your yokes. I cast down wicked imaginations in the name of Jesus Christ.

In the name of Jesus, I break all ungodly spiritual contracts that were made in times of fear and desperation, out of ignorance, manipulation and greed; In the name of Jesus Christ, these ungodly contracts are now null and void. Satan you no longer have rights to me, my children (my grandchildren and their children and their children), my parents, my siblings, my nieces, nephews and cousins; your rights have been revoked in Jesus' name.

In the name of Jesus, I bind that wicked spirit of oppression. You will no longer torment us with past fears and failures. No longer will you hinder or limit our progress, nor will you steal from us or attempt to destroy my family anymore; your rights have been revoked. I command you to cease your attacks right now in the name of Jesus Christ.

In the name of Jesus Christ, I rebuke the spirit of premature death. We will not die before our time. We will live and declare the works of the Lord, we will live a life of purpose, an abundant life, the ZOE life.

In the name of Jesus, we are healed emotionally, mentally and spiritually. We are financially stable, we are financially wealthy, we are lenders, not borrowers. We are the head, not the tail. We are a sound people in the Mighty name of Jesus Christ. Father God, I ask from this day onward, let your blessings and provisions flow freely in the lives of my sisters, brothers, nieces, nephews, cousins and life-time friends in the great name of Jesus. AMEN, AMEN, AMEN.

CHAPTER 11

Break the Curse: Finances

Finances:

If you find yourself dealing with financial deficit/difficulties repeat this prayer:

Father God in the name of Jesus Christ, I lay my burden at your feet... Lord Jesus Christ, according to your Word, those that trust in you will not be made ashamed. As I commit my thoughts to you, thank you for establishing the works of my hands causing me to prosper financially. just like you caused Isaac to prosper in the time of famine, thank you for my financial provision coming forth as I sow in my time, in my profession, in Jesus name. Your Word, Lord God says "to prove" you now as I bring my tithes into your storehouse. Thank you for opening the windows of Heaven and for pouring out a blessing that I do not have enough room to receive it.

Thank you for rebuking the devourer for my sake, for causing my vines to bear fruit in due season. Causing wealth and riches to dwell in my household. I am a delightsome land, where you are continually glorified.

Thank you, Lord God for taking pleasure in my prosperity. Thank you, Lord Jesus, for causing me to walk in the fullness of Abraham's blessings: divine guidance, divine protection, and divine provision. My children and their children and their children and many generations are blessed beyond measure.

I thank you Father God... In the matchless name of Jesus Christ, I pray. AMEN! AMEN! AMEN

CHAPTER 12

Break the Curse: Poverty

Poverty:

If you find yourself dealing with poverty pray this prayer:

Father God in the mighty name of Jesus Christ, I break the curse of POVERTY that has been spoken against me, I break the curse of premature death in the mighty name of Jesus Christ. Every curse of financial lack, limitations, discrimination, failure in marriages and families, failure in ministry, in the mighty name of Jesus Christ, I break the curse of poverty. In the mighty name of Jesus Christ, I bind that thief. No longer will you steal from me. No longer will you kill my hopes and dreams. No longer will you attempt to destroy my life. In the mighty name of Jesus Christ, I arrest that spirit of jealousy and envy.

No longer will you meddle in the affairs of my life. In Jesus Name, AMEN! AMEN! AMEN!

CHAPTER 13

Break the Curse: Restoration

Restoration:

If you find yourself dealing with loss repeat this prayer:

Father God in the name of Jesus Christ, I call on your name, Jehovah Jireh, for you are my priest, my protector, and my provider. I know, those that trust in you will not be made ashamed. I thank you, Lord Jesus Christ, for turning my mourning into dancing, for girding me with the garment of praise, not sorrow. Lord Jesus, your Word states "What the thief has stolen he must return... he must give back what he has stolen seven times more."

Therefore, in the name of Jesus Christ, I command that thief to return what rightfully belongs to me: return the finances, the properties opportunities, promises that were stolen, return them NOW! IN THE NAME OF JESUS CHRIST!

I call forth divine recompense to come forth into my life in the name of Jesus Christ. I thank you Father God for restoring what the canker worms and palmer worms have eaten. I thank you for your will being done in my life on earth as it is in Heaven. I thank you Father God that my latter days are greater than my former days. God, I thank you for the plans that you have for me, plans of hope, plans with an expected end. Thank you for divine restoration. In your Son Jesus' name. AMEN! AMEN! AMEN!

CHAPTER 14

Break the Curse: Healing

Healing:

If you find yourself in need of a healing pray this prayer:

Father God, in the name of Jesus Christ, I come before you Jehovah Rapha, believing you for divine healing, for healing is the children's bread. I thank you Lord Jesus Christ. By your stripes I am physically healed, I am emotionally healed, and I am spiritually healed. I thank you Jehovah Rapha for setting me free from the spirit of infirmity. By your stripes Lord God, I am healed from every sickness and disease. Thank you for every internal organ functioning in its full capacity. Thank you, Father God, for every cell reproducing normally in the name of Jesus, for every joint and limb made whole. I choose to believe you for my divine healing, just like you healed the woman with the issue of blood. Just like you healed the ten lepers. Thank you, Lord Jesus Christ, for healing my body, healing my mind from every curse that has been spoken against me.

I will not die but live and declare the works of the Lord. Father God, thank you for long life, even in my old age I will be fruitful, functioning in the right state of mind. I will live a full and satisfying life in your name Jesus Christ. AMEN! AMEN! AMEN!

CHAPTER 15

Break the Curse: Hindrances

Hinderances:

If you find yourself dealing with hinderances, pray this prayer:

Father God in the name of Jesus Christ I call on your name, Jehovah Nissi, you are the Great I Am, The God Almighty. Thank you, Lord Jesus Christ, for going before me, for making every crooked path straight. Thank you for breaking asunder every bar of brass that was meant to imprison me and hold hostage my blessing, the answers to my prayers. Thank you for rebuking the works of Satan, the opposer that is causing a hinderance, a blockage, to my progress, to my breakthrough. I refuse to digress. I refuse to regress. I refuse to give up. Therefore, in your name, Lord Jesus, I rebuke the spirit of discouragement. I am strong, and I am courageous

I am more than a conqueror. I am an overcomer. I am moving forward in your name, Lord Jesus. I am walking in the footsteps that you have laid before me. I will walk on the paths that you have prepared for me; Guided by your Holy Spirit, moving at an accelerated pace. In Jesus name. **AMEN! AMEN! AMEN!**

CHAPTER 16

Redemptive Power: Seven Promises

God's Seven Promises:

Father God in the Mighty name of Jesus Christ, I thank you for giving your angels charge over me. Thank you for your divine guidance. I thank you Father God for divine protection, for taking over this warfare against my adversaries.

Because you are my shepherd I shall not want; every need will be met. Thank you for divine provision. Thank you for deliverance from the many afflictions, for lifting the burdens and releasing the pains.

I thank you Father God for renewing my strength that I may be fruitful in my old age.

Thank you, Father God, for releasing an anointing of abundance over me this year Father God. In Jesus name AMEN! AMEN! AMEN!

CHAPTER 17

Redemptive Power: The Lord's Prayer

The Lord's Prayer:

Matthew 6:9-13 New International Version (NIV)
[9] "This, then, is how you should pray:

"'Our Father in heaven,
hallowed be your name,
[10] your kingdom come,
your will be done,
 on earth as it is in heaven.
[11] Give us today our daily bread.
[12] And forgive us our debts,
 as we also have forgiven our debtors.
[13] And lead us not into temptation,
 but deliver us from the evil one.'

CHAPTER 18

Redemptive Power: Overcoming Witchcraft

Prayer:

If you find yourself dealing with witchcraft repeat this prayer:

Father God, in the name of Jesus Christ, I proclaim that I am liberated in you. In the name of Jesus Christ, I am free from every form of Black Magic, every spell and work of voodoo, and every enchantment. I am are free from the spirit of fear, hopelessness and despair.
    In the name of Jesus Christ, I am strengthened in my inner man in the might of God's power. In the name of Jesus Christ, the spirit of my mind is renewed after the Word of God. My mind is sound and sober, my sight and vision are clear. Father God, fill me afresh with

your Holy Spirit. I plead the blood of Jesus Christ upon everyone that is attached to me.

Thank you, Father God, for your truth. Who the Son sets free is free indeed. Thank you, Father God, for setting me free from the works of witchcraft, from the influence of the Jezebel spirit, and from the lies spoken by false prophets. In the name of Jesus Christ, I pray. AMEN! AMEN! AMEN!

"There's no god, like Jehovah!"

EPILOGUE

NEW BEGINNINGS

The Power Points of Spiritual Warfare

Day 1: Journal your prayers:

The Power Points of Spiritual Warfare

Day 2: Journal your prayers:

The Power Points of Spiritual Warfare

Day 3: Journal your prayers:

The Power Points of Spiritual Warfare

Day 4: Journal your prayers:

The Power Points of Spiritual Warfare

Day 5: Journal your prayers:

The Power Points of Spiritual Warfare

Day 6: Journal your prayers:

The Power Points of Spiritual Warfare

Day 7: Journal your prayers:

BIBLIOGRAPHY

Research:

Witchcraft:

Dereck Prince: witchcraft in your church online publication November 22, 2015

Bishop George Bloomer: Spiritual Authority/ Witchcraft in the pews published in 1995, online publication Oct 10, 2015

Bishop T D Jakes- Spell Breaker published Mar 24, 2014; www.tdjakes.org

Arch- Bishop Nicholas Duncan-Williams Action Chapel International ministry: The ongoing war Published Aug 9, 2018

The Spirit of Jezebel:
Apostle Ryan LA Strange: Unusual Vindication 7/12/18,

Jezebel, The Spiritual Assassin, April 25, 2018, Exit the House of Saul June 27, 2017,

The Spirit of Sabotage Against Divine Alignments December 28, 2017, 3 ingredients for Next Level May 23, 2017

Pastor Robert Morris: Stop tolerating Jezebel Spirit

Spiritual Discernment and Controlling churches: Apostle John Eckhardt: Crusaders Church in Chicago, Ill. Discerning of spirit challenges online publication May 14, 2018,

www.johneckhardt.global, Deliverance from a controlling Spirit online publication Oct 14, 2014, Strongholds:

Intercessory Prayer:

Prophet Vincent K. Kpodo: Midnight Prayers published on Facebook live and Periscope

Prophet Brian Carn: Prophetic Encounters; There has been a security breach; Momentum Sunday- December 6, 2015 World Harvest Church Pastor Rod Parsley;

Pastor Robert Clancy: Deliverance

Cited Articles:

John Corn: Spiritual Husbands and Spiritual Wives

Arch Bishop Dunkin-Williams***

ABOUT THE AUTHOR

Pastor Tawana T. Thomas has been chosen for such a time as this. She has a spirit of boldness and a willingness to fight the good fight of faith without fear that represents the foundation of who she is in Christ. She is fondly called the World-Renowned Diva of the Kingdom of God. She is willing to wrestle until a breakthrough emerges. She will not give up on her assignment until God gets the glory, and she teaches the people of God to have faith to obtain the same power and anointing as well.

A well-trained minister, Tawana was tutored for ministry under the leadership and guidance of Pastor William Statham of Unto Full Stature Holiness Church. Pastor Thomas believes serving begins at home. She has been actively involved in ministry for over 19 years, particularly with the Christian Education department and the Missions department at church because the Lord has instilled in her heart the mandate to feed His sheep. Pastor Tawana T. Thomas was ordained as an Independent Christian clergy in November

2012 by Rev. D. E. McElroy (World Christian Ministry).

The Lord has divinely connected her with individuals who have encouraged, supported, prayed and worked with her so that she is equipped to pave the way forward. Pastor Tawana T. Thomas has served as a guest cohost in Christian Media. She is the creator of tawanathomas.com and Power Point International Ministry. Pastor Tawana has also hosted numerous workshops dealing with relationships, women, finances, entrepreneurship, and other relevant topics.

A single parent of two wonderful, handsome, young men, she recognizes that they are very supportive of her endeavors.

She is a graduate of Saint Peter's University, where she began her theological studies. She has earned certificates in Biblical Studies, Pastoral Counseling and Church History, and has also earned a Bachelor of Science degree in Business Administration. Tawana's career began in the financial industry. She is also involved in the public-school district; believing every child has a right to fair education. Tawana recognizes that her parents, the late Mr. and Mrs. Ivory Thomas, prayed for her and prepared her to honor God's plan for her life. Dr. Renee Hornbuckle of Destiny Pointe Christian Fellowship in Arlington, Texas introduced Tawana T. Thomas to the platform of her destiny. Finally, without her professors, teachers, family and friends, she would not be the world renowned, divinely inspired, virtually anointed woman of God that she is today!

You can connect with Pastor Tawana T. Thomas on Social Media:

Website: tawanathomas.com

Facebook: Tawana T Thomas@Royality17

Instagram: tawanatthomas

ORDER INFORMATION

You can order additional copies of Power Points of Overcoming Witchcraft by emailing the author directly using the email address below.

Tawana T. Thomas

Email Address:

tawana_thomas@rocketmail.com

Books are available at Amazon.com, Kindle and Your Local Bookstores (By Request)

Please leave a review for this book on Amazon and let other readers know how much you enjoyed reading it.

Thank you!

www.ingramcontent.com/pod-product-compliance
Lightning Source LLC
Chambersburg PA
CBHW071136090426
42736CB00012B/2138